ІСТОРІЯ ЧИСЕЛ

THE NUMBER STORY

SMALL BOOK ONE

ENGLISH - UKRAINIAN

Numbers Teach Children
Their Number Names

written and illustrated by

MISS ANNA

Early Reader Edition of *The Number Story 1*
Bronze Medal Winner, 2016 Wishing Shelf Book Award

Library of Congress Control Number: 2018902040

Names: Miss Anna, author.
Title: Number story : numbers teach children their number names / Miss Anna.
Description: Portland, OR: Lumpy Publishing, 2018.
Identifiers: ISBN 978-1-945977-54-1 | LCCN 2018902040
Summary: The pictures and rhymes present stories which introduce numbers 0-10.
Subjects: LCSH Numeration—English--Ukrainian--Pictorial works--Juvenile literature. | BISAC JUVENILE NONFICTION /
Languages: English--Ukrainian
Classification: LCC QA141.3 .M57 2018 | DDC 513—dc23

Publisher: Lumpy Publishing
Website: www.missannabooks.com
Email: missanna@missannabooks.com
Facebook: Miss Anna Lumpy

Paperback: ISBN 978-1-945977-54-1
Printed in the U.S.A.   1 3 5 7 9 10 8 6 4 2

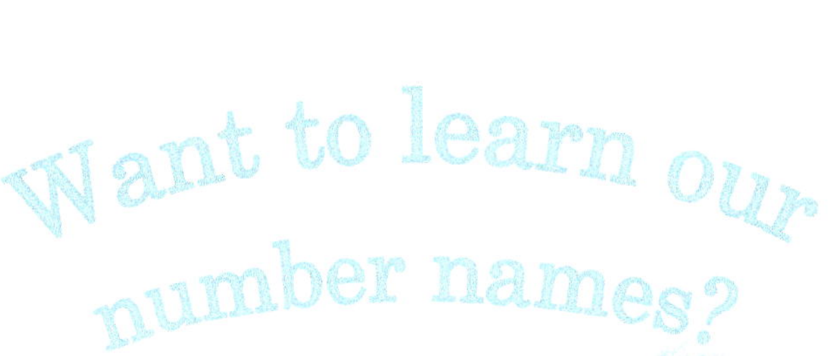

Want to learn our number names?

Хочеш вивчити назви чисел?

It is very easy and a lot of fun!

Це дуже просто і весело!

Say-along our little jingle

Заспівай цю маленьку
історію разом з нами!

starting from Number One!

Начнем из цифры один!

ONE looks like my one finger.

Один

Схоже на Один мій пальчик.

ONE!

Один!

2

TWO trails a tail.

Два

У Два є хвостик.

A TAIL! ХВОСТИК!

3

THREE has bumps.

ТРИ

Три має пагорби.

ПАГОРБИ!
Поглянь на зелені пагорби!

4

FOUR carries a sail.

ЧОТИРИ

Чотири тримає парус.

A SAIL!

ПАРУС!
Човен з парусом!

5

FIVE is a racing track.

П'ЯТЬ

П'ять – гоночна доріжка.

VROOM
ВРУММ!
1

SIX curves like a snail.

ШІСТЬ

Шість скрутилося, як равлик.

A SNAIL! РАВЛИК!

7

SEVEN has a sharp angle.

СІМ

Сім має гострий кут.

OUCH!
ОЙ!

8

EIGHT   is rollercoaster rails.

ВІСІМ

Вісім – це американські гірки.

йухууу!
YIPPEE!

NINE is a bubble on a stick.

ДЕВ'ЯТЬ

Дев'ять – це бульбашка

на паличці.

A BUBBLE! БУЛЬБАШКА!

10

TEN is an eye of a whale.

ДЕСЯТЬ

Десять — це око кита.

HELLO!   ПРИВІТ!

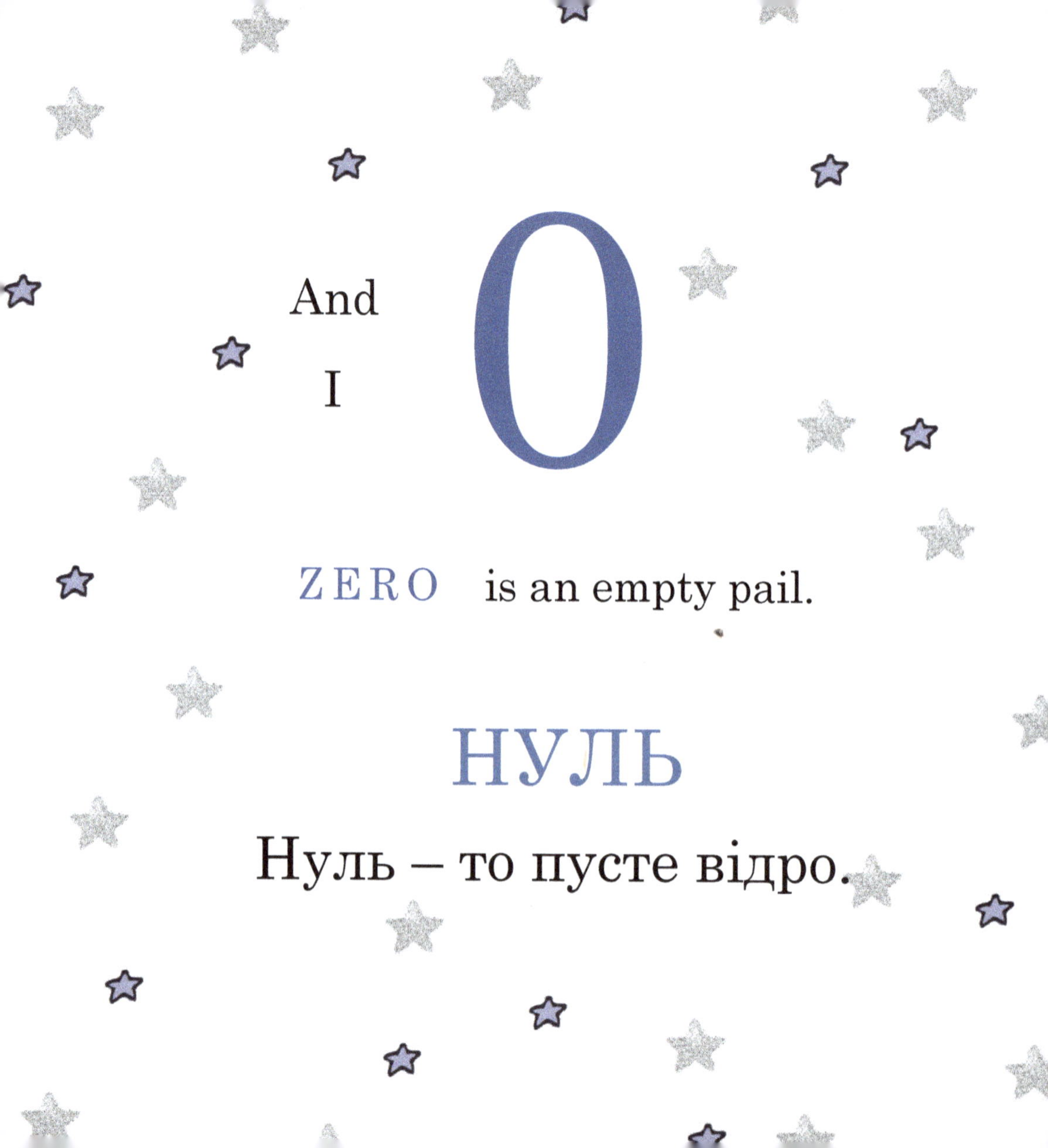

And I **0**

ZERO is an empty pail.

НУЛЬ

Нуль – то пусте відро.

IT'S EMPTY!
Воно пусте!

Thank you for playing with us today.

We had a lot of fun too!

Дякуємо за те, що

пограли з нами сьогодні.

Нам теж було дуже весело!

We are your Number friends,
Zero to Ten,
Who will be here for you~

Ми ваші друзі

Від Нуля до Десяти.

Ми завжди будемо поруч із тобою.

Bye-bye now!
See you again soon!

А зараз прощавай!

Невдовзі побачимося!

The Numbers are *SINGING* too!

To sing-a-long, look for Miss Anna Number Story
at your favorite music store like iTUNES.

MP3

Numbers 0-10
IDENTIFYING
& COUNTING

Numbers 11-20
& Ordinals

first, second, third...

Numbers 0-100
& Place Values

ones, tens, hundreds...

About Clocks
& Telling Time

hours, minutes, seconds

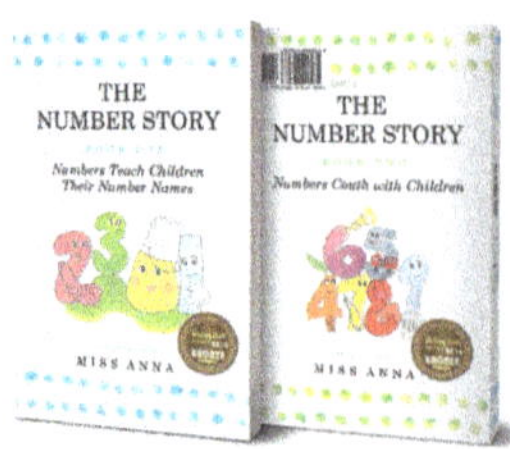

Number Story 1 & 2

isbn: 978-0-996216-48-7

Number Story 3 & 4

isbn: 978-1-945977-01-5

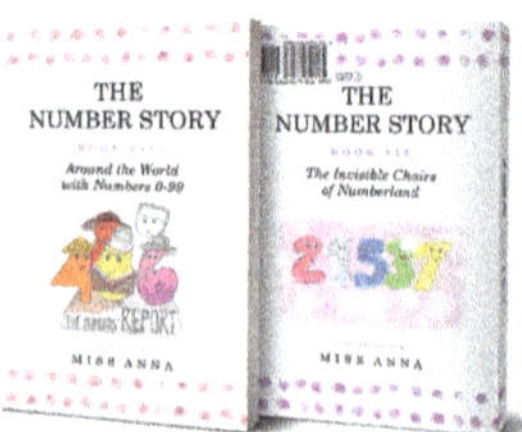

Number Story 5 & 6

isbn: 978-1-945977-06-0

Number Story 7 & 8

isbn: 978-1-949320-40-4

For more Miss Anna books to love,
visit us at

www.missannabooks.com

Numbers are working hard all over the world!
Come Travel the World with Us!

www.ingramcontent.com/pod-product-compliance
Lightning Source LLC
Chambersburg PA
CBHW040900070726
47599CB00035B/2247